Sonti

60 Years of Blood, Sweat, Tears, and Joy!

**The Autobiography of
Ntsayi Letesia Sonti Ledwaba**

SEED WORD
COMMUNICATIONS
Joshua 1:9
Colossians 3:23

Sonti: 60 Years of Blood, Sweat, Tears, and Joy!
Copyright ©2010 by Ntsayi Letesia Sonti Ledwaba

ISBN 978-0-9817603-1-5
Library of Congress Control Number: 2010940669

Published by:
Seed Word Communications
P.O. Box 16615
Tallahassee, FL 32317
Phone: +1.850.893.9781
www.seedword.com

Cover design by Ruth Palao
rpvdesigns@gmail.com

Copyediting, interior design and production by
Alan Prescott
www.prescottdesignshop.com
prescott_alan@comcast.net
alanjayprescott@gmail.com

Foreword

I never dreamed in a million years that I would become an author. However, I firmly believe that everything happens for a reason. About two years ago, I met a gentleman from the United States of America—in a hairdressing salon of all places. He said he was visiting South Africa on a short business trip and gave me his business card. I am convinced that it was not by coincidence that we met again on a few other occasions at the same salon and began sharing conversations about our backgrounds. I learned that he was a public speaker and would be willing to do a leadership seminar for my management team some day in the future. I also found out that he owned a book publishing company in America after he gave me some samples of his books.

One of the books was about the amazing story of the life of a young lady from the Kingdom of Lesotho titled *The King's Daughter from Lesotho*. After reading that book, I told him that the story sounded very much like mine. He encouraged me to consider writing my own autobiography, saying that he believed the younger generation of South African women could learn some valuable lessons from my life experiences. He also said that many African-Americans would be interested in reading about life experiences in their motherland. He kept pushing me, and after I retired from civil service a year later I started writing.

In the beginning, I was very nervous because I have always been a very assertive but private person and had never shared my personal story or feelings publicly. I only began to enjoy it after I wrote a few pages. I have poured out my heart in this tale. Sometimes, I felt that I was washing my dirty linen in public, but he encouraged me not to hold anything back. He said I should be brutally honest and not sugar-coat any of my stories. Therefore, the accounts here are exactly as they occurred. Some are embarrassing and others even shameful, but overall, they make me quite proud of my accomplishments. If my story provokes a positive thought or inspires even just one person to find deeper meaning in life, I will feel that my time was not wasted.

I am eternally grateful for that stranger from America, Dr. Joseph Amanfu, who has now become like my true blood brother.

Ntsayi Letesia Sonti Ledwaba

Dedication

I dedicate this book to my late mom, Mamlini and dad, Josiah, who I regret are not alive to see their daughter make it through life with blood, sweat, tears and joy.

Table of Contents

CHAPTER 1

Sonti:
The First Child

Being the firstborn in a family of nine children presented me with extraordinary challenges, opportunities and responsibilities. I was born on the 10th of October, 1948—a holiday known as Kruger Day—during the time of apartheid. On that day in 1825, the famous South African statesman Stephanus Johannes Paul Kruger was born in Colesberg, Cape Colony. He became the president of the Transvaal Republic.

When the African National Congress [ANC] came into power, that holiday was abolished, denying me the special opportunity of celebrating my birthday on a national holiday.

Sonti is a nickname, a Tswana language version of the Zulu name Sonto, which means Sunday or holiday. According to the original black South

African custom, all first children are expected to be born at the mother's home, even if she was married. My maternal grandmother gave me the name Sonti because of the holiday, and my father's people gave me the name Ntsayi. Nobody knows the meaning of the name, but it was the name of my paternal grandmother's sister.

My late mother, Manlini Merica Zwane, was originally from Kwa-Zulu Natal and very distinctly Zulu. My late father, Mothopi Josiah Mokgako, was of Tswana origin. His family came from Kgwadibeng (Kwa-Mosetlhe) in Hammanskraal, then moved to Marapyane in Northern Pretoria. They then stayed briefly at Withok, Brice and Enkelbos farms near Springs before finally settling in Payneville, Springs, east of Johannesburg in the Transvaal. This final location was where my father grew up.

When I was growing up, my paternal grandparents had a house at 1373 18th Avenue in Payneville, Springs. My paternal grandfather was a businessman selling fine wood. It was a pleasure to visit during school days.

Who Really is Sonti?

My birth maiden name is Mokgako. Everyone born in the Mokgako family has been identified with the specific traditional praise entitled "*Motho Wa Bo Mokgako.*" The full traditional praise is printed below:

KGOMO, MOKGAKO OA THIBEDI.KE

*LERUMO LE LEGOLO NKGERE LE
NTSENG LE FERELETSA MATEBELE.
NKGERE KA NTSHA TSHOSA KA BATA
LEPONO LAGA MOKGAJANE. BA RE
NTJAU O THLAGILE A TSHWERE MO-
LETSE WA MOTHO: A OFA RANKORO:
RANKORO A O GANA : A RE OMPHA
MOLETSE WA MOTHO TLHANG WA
SUGU LA KGOMO WA LE NTIMA.*

The expressions do not have an accurate translation or equivalent in English, but at the risk of compromising the depth in cultural meaning, the words would mean the following:

Kgomo is a cow, so we identify with a cow. *Lerumo le legolo nkgere* means a big spear brandished to scare away enemies. At the same time that one goes through the list of my late grandfathers and great-grandfathers, their names are also reflected in the praise: Ntjhau was the father to my paternal grandfather while Nkgere was one of his brothers.

Most South African tribes have their unique style of traditional praises that are narrated at all special occasions, such as weddings, funerals and other celebrations. These expressions are called *direto* in my native Tswana language and *izibongo* in Zulu. Whenever these words are recited, the women present must ululate in response. Ululating sounds like the "li...li...li...li" sound and is made without allowing gaps—it is stretched for as long as the breath can sustain, depicting pride, happiness or joy.

My Paternal Grandparents

My late paternal grandmother, Motlhagudi Wilhemina Mokgako, died at age 86 after turning blind for six months. I was then a teenager and used to visit her during school holidays. My late paternal grandfather, Nehemiah Ramothupi Mokgako, was a businessman selling firewood as I grew up. He had three horses named Prince, March and Esther, and used a horse cart to load wood every morning to sell in town. At night, there would be a fire made in the courtyard where wood was chopped and packed in bags ready to be loaded for selling early the next day. During the chopping there would be a lot of socialization, the sharing of jokes and teasing each other among the grandchildren from his varied offspring. We would be spoiled with white bread, jam and tea made with fresh milk. At my home we normally ate brown bread with peanut butter, and tea with condensed milk, so this was luxury.

My late grandfather reportedly built his business from money earned after returning from fighting wars as a South African soldier. He died at an estimated age of 120 years while I was at university. My father hailed from a family of five children.

My Maternal Grandparents

My late maternal grandmother was Annie Phambekile Zwane. As I grew up she was working at the Vryheid Provincial Hospital laundry until retirement age. She was born around 1889 and died in

1974 at the age of 85.

She also spoiled us during school holidays, always something nice after work. We actually ran to meet her at the bus stop after work. She bought a lot of meat, and we were allowed to eat as much as we could.

My late maternal grandfather died when my mother was still young, so we never got to know him. He had also apparently participated in South African wars as a soldier. My late mother came from a family of 13 children.

We were a family of nine children, but the fourth and fifth children died before reaching two and three years, respectively. I know that one of them died of measles. I am not very sure, but I think the second one died of measles as well. For most of this time, we grew up in a family of seven children, four boys and three girls.

We had all believed that I was the first child of both my father and mother until only recently, when we began to hear rumors that my father had made a girl pregnant prior to meeting my mother. Because of family disputes and attitudes, my father's family did not approve of that relationship. There was, therefore, a disconnection between the two families. The expectant girl was relocated and, up to my father's death, there was never any contact. Unfortunately, my father passed away in 1987 before this allegation surfaced and thus never had the opportunity to deny or confirm the rumor. The mystery remains unsolved.

Returning to how I grew up, I was regarded as an extra-precious gift and very overprotected. I was not allowed to make mistakes and never went out to play with my peers. I actually never played, and I still suffer the consequences up to this day. I cannot go to the gym because I fear falling. I do not go on escalators and cannot swim, although I have a swimming pool. I do not get into the sea. No boats, no heights, no merry go-rounds. The list is seemingly endless. I have never played in any sport and was punished at school for not participating. But all I needed was for them to understand and assist me instead of punishing me. The damage is indelible and irreparable, and cannot be erased or wished away.

I was very quiet, schooled to be seen and not heard. I had to be a real trendsetter and an example of perfect upbringing. If one of my siblings cried, I had to know why he or she cried. If they fell, I would take the blame for it. I had to help with the household chores at an early age and assist in looking after the younger siblings.

My mother was also very quick in slapping us backward and forward. A clap on the head or face was a daily routine that caused me to withdraw internally. That behavior earned me the description of being quiet or sweet—a paragon of perfection!

My early school days were characterized by quietude, absentmindedness, oblivion and distraction. I was perceived as a slow learner by some of my teachers and things only turned around when I was in Standard 5 (now Grade 7) when I had become an "A" student.

I think my bed-wetting was caused by the climate that prevailed at my home during my early childhood. I never showed my true self and did not feel relaxed most of the time. I was a quiet, programmed child. I devote a chapter later in this book to this problem and how my parents dealt with it.

The early school-going days were a nightmare for me. My mother was a teacher at the same school, so I faced her strictness in both places. Although I was never in my mother's classes, any mistake observed by any teacher would mean a trip to go and tell my mother.

If I failed a test, skipped doing my homework or did anything else wrong, I was sent flying to go and report myself to my mother. She would obviously scream and yell at me with the additional insult of a slap in the face or on the head, the latter being her favorite target.

I hated school at that stage. In fact, I hardly knew why I went to school. My teacher in Standard 1 was also very harsh, a screamer who used a cane to beat up students. We had to open both hands face up, and that was hell. I applaud the people who recently abolished corporal punishment at school. During this time, I just lived life as it unfolded, but had nothing exciting going on.

Home was not cozy. I had no friends. I continued being regarded as quiet and obedient. I was not even allowed to befriend older people, let alone my age group. So there was no environment for venting my feelings. There was strict law and order. Our teachers commanded respect and even created fear in some cases.

I was fortunate that there were a few positives about being a first child, for instance, respect from my younger siblings. One good example was that when I started menstruating, I was given a bedroom to share with my two sisters, while my four brothers had to sleep in the dining room. My home was designed to be a three-room house, with the kitchen and dining room being an open plan. My parents partitioned the two rooms to be separate, transforming our house into a four-room, semi-detached house. Our section of the house was 10390A, while the other half, 10390B, was occupied by another family.

Our dining room was used as a bedroom at night and all the furniture had to be shifted to some corner.

Our dining room was used as a bedroom, so all the furniture had to be shifted to some corner every night. Anybody visiting after dark was forced to come in through the kitchen door and sit in the kitchen or be spoken to through one of the windows in the house. The four-room home, therefore, accommodated nine people. Of course, my parents occupied one bedroom, the girls slept in the other, and the boys were assigned the dining room floor. Fortunately, most of the visitors were either kids or relatives. If they were males, they had to join the boys and females had to join the girls. Though visitors were an inconvenience, we always had them, especially during school holidays.

There was mutual respect for one another's privacy, despite the small size of our house. We bathed ourselves in washing basins in the bedrooms and never undressed publicly. Decency was maintained at all times.

My mother's strictness actually helped me to decide quickly whether to go to boarding school or local high school for further learning. I did not know how boarding school life would be, but I told myself that it would emancipate me from a home environment that was strict and authoritative.

The boarding school fees were a donation from the Catholic Church, which ran the same school where my mother taught and I attended. Four of us from the school were selected to go to a Catholic boarding school and we did not pay fees. The arrangements were between the parish priest in the school and the receiving boarding school.

In my case, the opportunity was given because I had been successful at school and also well-behaved. I obtained a first-class pass in Standard 6. Another factor was that my mother taught at a school where I was a student and the teachers grossly underpaid. I was convinced that the opportunity to attend a boarding high school for free was a God-given breakthrough and did not take it lightly. I worked hard and excelled academically. I took a negative situation and turned it into an opportunity that yielded positive results. It was a turning point in my life from which I never looked back.

I used unpleasant factors such as a big family and a disciplined, rigid upbringing to turn my life around for the good. I made resolutions such as:

> I will invest in self-development
>
> I will work hard to stay out of poverty
>
> I will only have one or two children
>
> I will befriend and bond with them
>
> I will provide better accommodation for them so that they have their own bedrooms
>
> I will ensure that they have a good education

The wish list was almost endless, but I am glad to report that I have been able to do all the things on it with one exception: none of my children became university graduates, even though I have a postgraduate qualification and occupied senior positions in my career.

My daughter is intellectually challenged and my son dropped out of Technikon. He did, however, go for computer training, and the skills acquired helped him to be employed. He seems to enjoy what he is doing and I am very proud of him. He has neither been unemployed nor in trouble with the law. I am very happy with my two children and gratified that I now have a daughter-in-law and a grandson. At this stage, I feel self-actualized.

The relationship with my mother also changed as she grew older. I suspect that she might have simmered down because of all the children that she had to raise. As a result of my having stayed away from home through boarding schools, university and marriage, the relationship changed and the bond strengthened. I also noticed that with my younger siblings growing up, the strictness stopped. Some of them actually do not believe that my mother was ever harsh or strict at any point. What was more unbelievable was to watch how she spoiled her grandchildren.

She was the most lovable and loving mother, grandmother and wife. She had become a friend, especially to my sisters and me. My experience with her during my early childhood days is like a fairytale. The later years were so enjoyable and rich that memories about my mother are only beautiful ones. My son also enjoyed her warmth and love because—prior to her death—she stayed with all her grandchildren. After the funeral, it was sad for each of us to bundle up our children and their baggage. Anyway, we got used to it. Today, most of these grandchildren have their own families, but never stop talking about their grandmother; they cherish fond memories of her.

I imagine that my mother also had her own frustrations in the early years, having to take care of and provide for so many youngsters. Bringing up and caring for children can be quite stressful. I suppose I had to have my own in order to understand and fully appreciate her challenges: being a working mother of nine children and losing two. My mother had no domestic helper to assist her. Teaching added the difficulties of completing schoolwork at home, at the same time she had the duties of housework and being a mother and wife.

My perception of my father was that he was the soft one. During my early development I was more comfortable with him. However, since my mother was always present at home, there was no opportunity for bonding with him. I remember him as a loving and handsome man with a beautiful smile. He was also a very friendly and humble person.

I would sing "The Lord Is My Shepherd" whenever my father was in a good mood and asked me to sing. It all started in school when I was in Grade 7, at about 14 years old. The class teacher was very musical and I was in the class choir. A soprano, I was selected together with another classmate to sing solos whenever we performed "The Lord Is My Shepherd" at school.

Those were some of the small things that began to shape my self-esteem. My father showed his pride by asking me to sing, giving me great encouragement. Whenever he had friends over for dinner, the dessert he served was asking his little girl to come and sing. The compliments from him and the guests always increased my confidence.

This emboldened me to join choirs wherever I went. I was a member of the choirs at my boarding school, and later on I sang in the university choir. Even now, I am a member of my church choir. Perhaps if I had not followed the academic path, I might have had a career in music. Singing is still one of my most enjoyable hobbies and lifts my spirit. I am able to sing my sorrows away and also express my joy through a song.

Whenever I hear the song "The Lord Is My Shepherd" it brings me fond memories, and I reminisce about those lucky moments when my father gave me encouragement and expressed his appreciation of my singing talent. I wish all parents would help to identify the God-given gifts in their children. What a wealthy world this would be! The following are the words of my favorite Psalm of David:

> [1]The Lord is my shepherd, I shall not
> be in want.
>
> [2]He makes me lie down in green pas-
> tures,
> He leads me beside quiet waters,
>
> [3]He restores my soul.
> He guides me in paths of righteousness
> for His Name's sake.
>
> [4]Even though I walk through the valley
> of the shadow of death, I will fear no
> evil, for You are with me; Your rod

and Your staff, they comfort me.

[5]You prepare a table before me in the
presence of my enemies. You anoint
my head with oil; my cup overflows.

[6]Surely goodness and love will follow
me all the days of my life, and I will
dwell in the house of the Lord forever.

Things have changed a lot these days. The belief
during former times was that the authoritative
family style was the best. Children had to be instructed and not asked or negotiated with. These
days, children are often consulted and they are allowed to express their opinions freely. They are
often able to make their own decisions. In the past,
a child could never leave home to stay on her own
except through marriage. Today, girls are allowed
to be independent, which in my view is a very positive change. Young women are now able to live on
their own and do very well with successful careers
and lifestyles.

After my mother's death, my father lived for only
a short period before moving on to join her in their
new residence in the land of our forefathers. My
mother died in 1984 and my father in 1987. He was
67 years old and had already started receiving Old
Age Pension. I loved my father and it hurt to see him
drown himself in sorrows with the memories of my
mother's death. He grew very lonely and his health
deteriorated. He read the Bible daily, but his mental
state did not improve. He died in a hospital with

cardiac problems, prostate cancer and mental con-
fusion.

One eternal fact remaining is that I was born
and bred in a decent home and will be forever
grateful to my parents.

CHAPTER 2

A Girl in a Neighborhood Full of Boys

Life was tough at times, but thanks to God I survived. I was not subjected to early sex, rape or teenage-pregnancy problems.

I grew up in a "township," in a four-room semi-detached house in a communal environment where neighbors interacted a lot. My parents were friends of the neighbors and there would be occasions throughout the day, especially weekends, where they met as couples and socialized over drinks, snacks or meals and held discussions. They had fun as married couples.

The neighborhood boys always knew the homes at which the parents would be gathering. They also knew the homes where young girls would be left alone. Often, when my parents left us and went to those gatherings, the boys would sneak into our house and play tricks with us. Sometimes, my mom and dad asked the older boys to keep an eye on us because our parents thought them always trustworthy.

On a regular basis, the boys would plead with me, trying to convince me to play the game of sex with them. They said it was only a game, but I could read their dirty minds. They never used force, but their sneaky, gentle coercion could have made it easier for me to fall prey. I was good at ducking and diving; running around tables and chairs; and even throughout the house to avoid touches, kisses or fondling. This was very uncomfortable for me, but I felt that I could not report any situation to my parents, since the boys were neither hostile nor did they get an opportunity to touch or fondle me. I was afraid that if I brought this to my parents' attention, they would think I was the one who had a perverted mind and that the boys meant no harm.

> *They said it was only a game, but I could read their dirty minds.*

When I hear reports nowadays of neighborhood boys, brothers and even fathers forcing themselves on girls, I realize that I was lucky all those young men I grew up with only approached me politely and never raped me. All I had to do was to say, "No" and keep running away. I started late with sex, compared to today's standards. What is important is that I was ready and conscious of what I was doing when it ultimately happened.

Being perceived as a beautiful and well-behaved girl in a neighborhood of so many boys was a real challenge. I thank God that I never got sexually involved with any of my tormenters. Some were older, and one simple, careless mistake by me would have been one too many.

CHAPTER 3

My Mother, My Savior!

I was nearly raped when I was ten years old, but thanks to my late mother, to whom I am eternally indebted, I escaped. She saved my life. A cousin of mine, who stayed with his parents in the same street with my family, came to my home around 2:00 one afternoon. About 20 years old, his name was Boy, and he was the only child of my parents' late cousins.

Boy passed me outside and got into my home through the kitchen door into the dining room where my parents were sitting with our neighbors. When he came out of the house, I was still outside in the backyard. We were not allowed to sit with adults when they conversed because they feared that we would listen to inappropriate adult stuff.

Boy told me that my mother had asked him for

some coal and that I had to accompany him so that I could bring it with me from his home. I went towards the steel box where we kept the coal in order to take a small bucket that we normally used to pick up coal to make fire in the stove in our kitchen. Boy told me not to take the container, as he would give me one.

I headed for the kitchen door to report to my mother that I was leaving with Boy for the coal as per her instructions and told him what my intention was. He said it was unnecessary, since it was her who had given the instruction. I had been taught never to leave the yard without reporting it, but my cousin forbade me to do so and looked at me with impatience. I thought I had no option but to follow him innocently. There was nothing suspicious about him to me or anybody who saw us walking up the street to his home. We did not talk. There was nothing to talk about and I was a very quiet child.

On arriving at Boy's home, I went straight to the coal box and he went into the house. Before I could do anything he called me into the house, saying he had something nice to give me. I went into the house and he locked the door. I started feeling uncomfortable and told him I wanted to leave. Not until we did the "white person's game"—bioscope style—he said. I felt I was in trouble and started crying. Boy threw me on the bed and throttled my neck. I felt his heartbeat and smelled the scent of sweat and unwashed body. I was scared!

Just at that time, I heard my mother's voice screaming, "Boy, Boy!" I tried to scream, but no voice came out. His hands tightened around my neck as my mother's voice grew louder. Screaming, shouting, banging or hitting doors and windows, running and screaming around the house. Boy looked very confused by the noise and left me. He opened the back door, scaled the fences (this I was told later) and ran away. My mother was now breaking windows at the front side of the house. She came straight to me, asking what Boy had done to me. She was terrified and asked questions without waiting for my answers. Tearful and in shock, I said he throttled my neck, but nobody believed me because they all thought I had been raped. My mother took me to the police station to report the case and then to the clinic, where it was confirmed that I had not been raped. Only my neck had bruises and scratches.

She was terrified and asked questions without waiting for my answers.

That was a narrow escape. I never saw Boy again after that incident, but later heard he was imprisoned for assaulting a neighbor, gouging out one of his eyes during the scuffle. I was also told that the neighbor shot and killed Boy after his release from prison. I know that as a Christian I am not supposed to feel happy about someone's death, but I told myself that Boy had gotten what he deserved. I call it good riddance! He had been eliminated and at least there was closure from my side.

I have forever been grateful to my mother for having been the most vigilant and perceptive parent. Five minutes' delay from her would have scarred my whole life.

I learned later that on that day, my mother went to look for me and found me missing. She immediately called my name, looked for me in the yard and went into the street asking people if they had seen me. When she was told that I was seen with Boy, she ran to his home to search there. That was a classic example of how an African lioness frees her cub from capture. I look at parents today, allowing their girls to roam and wander around unsupervised even at night, and always ask myself, "Where are the mothers?"

I wish parents, especially mothers, would recognize their crucial role in the prevention of child abuse and the practice of effective parenting, keeping in mind the notion "prevention is better than cure." Maybe all mothers of the world need to come to Africa and visit the natural game parks to observe how animals protect their offspring.

My late mother deserves an award as "Mother of the Century." Her actions on that day and other days had and still have lifelong ripple effects. I have been perceived as overprotective of my own children; but who would not be, after what I experienced? I would rather be perceived as overprotective than negligent.

CHAPTER 4

Township Challenges

I was married and staying in another township in Soweto when I visited my parents at our house in Mzimhlophe Township one evening. They were at home, together with my younger sister. My younger brother was reportedly at a house two streets away from ours. Since this was the township my sister and I grew up in, we felt it was safe to walk. There were also shops just around the corner. Just as we were approaching the corner next to the shops, a group of boys came running, appearing from nowhere, and grabbed us. My younger sister is the seventh and I am the first child, but I could not protect her.

The boys pointed us to the veldt, open barren land three streets away, indicating that they were taking us there. I told them I was a married woman, but they said they did not care; those are the very ones they like most. I gasped in disgust. There was no point in screaming because we were opposite closed shops. I was certain that the two of us would be raped. These guys looked very desperate and appeared to be on a mission. In fact, we were about to be gang-raped. The one holding me had bloodshot eyes and looked very hostile. His teeth appeared as if they had not been brushed in a decade. Pleading would have been a waste of time and energy. He really looked desperate and divine intervention seemed our only hope.

They say miracles never cease to happen, and indeed, one did. One of the boys whispered something to the others and we were immediately released. According to my sister, he had recognized her as a sibling of one of my brothers, whom they knew very well and for whom they had respect. She informed them that I was an older sister to that brother. I suspect that they realized they could not withstand the vengeance of my brother if he found out that they had raped his sisters. There could possibly have been a serious confrontation.

They say miracles never cease to happen, and indeed, one did.

That was a narrow escape from the hands of thugs. After that incident, I realized that a township remains a township, with both positive and negative elements. We should never take our security for granted and play it safe all the time. From that day onwards, I have exercised caution whenever I go to my hometown.

Whenever I hear of gang-rape incidents, I think back to that day of my near encounter. One of my younger brothers actually got seriously injured later for confronting some of the gang members about the incident. That was township life. "Survival of the fittest" was the name of the game.

CHAPTER 5

A Personal Humiliating Challenge

I had a bed-wetting problem from childhood up to my teenage years, and this was a very painful and embarrassing experience in my life. I am not sure when the problem started, but by the time I was aware of it, I was in the substandard classes or primary education up to high school level. This was from about 6 years old up to about 16. My full awareness of the problem came when I was in Grade 3. I was a clean and beautiful young lady, very quiet and reserved, but the bed-wetting problem killed my soul. It shattered me completely.

This problem exposed me to a lot of punishment from my mother, who saw it as being too lazy to wake up and use the chamber pot provided in the house. Our toilets were outhouses that could be dangerous to visit at night. The initial punishment from my mother included a good beating with a belt. In addition, I had to wash the blankets at that tender age, before going to school, which sometimes made me late. The third punishment was from the teacher, who would give me another thorough beating with a cane for tardiness.

This torture went on from day to day, month to month, year to year. The worst part was that my mother would openly verbalize this problem, and I was sure most of my friends knew about it. This really humiliated me. After finishing Grade 8, I went into a boarding school to earn my junior certificate education. I was regarded as one of the most intelligent students in the class, with an A-level performance, but here was this embarrassing bed-wetting problem that followed me to boarding school. I received warnings from the nuns, and ultimately my parents were called in. My father came.

This torture went on from day to day, month to month, year to year.

After the complaint to my father, he went to a pharmacist for assistance and was given a tablet to give to me. At that time I did not question anything but did as instructed. I did not ask any questions about the name or usage or what the tablet was meant to correct. I just gobbled it down and it worked like magic. I was cured of a disease I cannot name or describe, as I had not been taken to any doctor for a diagnosis. My heart goes out to those adults who have carried the problem of bed-wetting into adulthood. I know of married men who wet their beds even while sleeping with girl-friends or wives. Children are also being subjected to all sorts of punishment and humiliation because of this problem, which is seldom discussed openly in health circles.

All I can say is that it is a humiliating, demoralizing and dehumanizing experience. I am happy I got assistance. By the time I completed my matric education (final year of high school), I had moved to a new boarding school. This was a fresh and new beginning for me.

I thank the nuns for helping my parents realize that it was necessary to look for other interventions besides punishment. My self-esteem was rebuilt and I became the human being with the potential God had bestowed on me. I never looked back except to take stock of the journey I traveled to be where I am today. This is my 60th year in life and I feel self-fulfilled. I could not have asked for more from my Creator as I followed His plan for my life.

I do not begrudge my mother for how she handled the situation. She did what she thought was best at that time. The experience instilled a lot of understanding and the ability in me to empathize with people who share painful or embarrassing life experiences. All of them, good and bad, contribute to making us who we are in life. It is our response and reaction to those experiences that determine whether we end up as good or bad people.

CHAPTER 6

Steve Biko's Influence on Me

I am not sure if this was a consequence of apartheid, religion or God knows what else, but I was born into a culture that associated blackness with evil, ugliness and inferiority. I do not know where this came from, but it was definitely not from the family-socialization process. I do not remember my parents ever criticizing blackness in the family. Perhaps apartheid and religion contributed to cementing the feelings of worthlessness in blacks, because purity was depicted in church through white images or statues. Jesus Christ, the Virgin Mary, Joseph and all the great people in the Bible were depicted as whites. To a growing mind, those images instill a certain belief or ideology. Satan was shown as a black, ugly and evil character.

Away from religion, it was common to see 4-, 5-

and 6-year-olds playing games where beauty, power and authority were shown through playing the role of a white "madam" or "misses," and ordering black people around. One would wear high-heeled shoes borrowed from either moms or older sisters. Makeup, wigs and lipstick were the favorite accessories. The mindset was already established that we had to be white to be beautiful, successful and powerful.

During my high school years when I was at boarding school, it was common practice that, towards the holidays, we started treating our faces by applying skin-lightening face creams. We believed that this would make us look smart, light in complexion and different from our local black friends and peers. The practice continued until I had my face damaged by a skin-lightening cream that was new on the market. My face blackened to such an extent that I could not believe what I saw—it worsened daily each time I checked myself in the mirror. I had to go to skin specialists to have my face treated.

It was not until Steve Biko's black-consciousness movement that the "black is beautiful" concept was instilled. Biko's influence penetrated through all levels and all ranks, including myself. For me, the black-consciousness concept not only fostered a sense of feeling good about being black, it helped me to realize that even as a black female I had rights to self-determination and the ability to maximize my potential and self-actualization. It made me realize that being beautiful has nothing to do with color. I am convinced that my beauty has to do with who I am on the inside and my feeling good about who I am.

I deeply appreciate the values and outlook that were imparted by the black-consciousness surge. I am convinced that it shaped who I am today. I knew very little about politics, especially being a product of Catholic private schools, but I knew a lot about Steve Biko.

I hated skin-lightening creams after that. To this day, I only buy face creams that protect or revitalize my skin, especially my face, but not the ones that change my pigmentation.

I deeply appreciate the values and outlook that were imparted by the black-consciousness surge.

In Chapter 9 of Biko's book *A Selection of His Quotations*, in his definition of black consciousness, he wrote, "It is a manifestation of a new realization that by seeking to run away from themselves and to emulate the white man, blacks are insulting the intelligence of whoever created them black. Black consciousness therefore, takes cognizance of the deliberateness of God's plan in creating black people black. I seek to infuse the black community with a new-found pride in themselves, their efforts, their value systems, their culture, religion and their outlook to life."

Thanks to Steve Biko, I am today proudly black. It was like music to my ears when in subsequent years I listened to people refer to me as a "black beauty." I love the song by the American soul legend James Brown titled "Say It Loud—I'm Black and I'm Proud."

God gave me a second chance because I have one of the most beautiful exteriors. My facial skin is healthy and revitalized, blemish- and wrinkle-free. It only sounds like a fabricated story when I tell people today that my face was once damaged, because there are no traces of the past.

CHAPTER 7

University Life

This was a big contrast and transition from life in the girls-only Catholic boarding schools I attended; they had been strict, very rigid and highly structured. In the Catholic school there was a daily program, from the specific time to wake up to the specific time to sleep.

We were required to wake up at 5:00 a.m. When the wake-up bell rang, we had to jump out of bed and kneel for prayer. After prayer, we ran to the shower rooms, washed, dressed up quickly and went for breakfast. It was necessary to pray before eating. Everything had to be done together in the group. After food, it was straight to classes, with lunch and tea breaks.

When classes were over, study times were structured. We all moved to the same venue and the nuns would monitor what we were studying by moving around the room and checking what each of us was reading.

If we had any letters to send to our families and friends, they were read by the nuns before being mailed. All incoming mail was also read by the nuns before delivery to us. All love letters were confiscated. It was a major transition from that type of restricted life to the freedom and independence at the university. At the university, we had to be self-driven, self-motivated and highly self-disciplined. No one either monitored whether one went to lectures or seemed to care whether one studied.

It was a major transition from that type of restricted life to the freedom and independence at the university.

This adjustment was very difficult for me. As much as I thought I was coping, I was shocked by the results, because I only passed one course during the first year. My parents were very disappointed, since up to that point I had been a straight-A-performance student. Even though I was determined to work harder, I knew that I could not complete my education within the three years for which I had funding. I did what I could and had to complete the rest of my degree by writing the psychology course after I left the university and started working.

The adjustment period during the first year of

university is what many students are not prepared for. Besides the challenge of managing my own time and academic studies, I had to adjust to life among male students. Some of them were befriending me, and some even confessed love and proposed future marriage.

My biggest challenge was that a love affair might result in a sexual relationship. This was very different from my ultraconservative, girls-only boarding school life where the mere mention of the word "sex" was taboo. Another challenge for me was the freedom of choosing what to wear at the university, since we wore only uniforms at the boarding school. I know my parents were glad that even though university life was challenging, I did not fall pregnant while there.

The maximum number of roommates at the university was three, compared to the 50 or 100 in the boarding school dormitory. Having pocket money at the Catholic boarding schools was not an issue because they did not allow luxurious lifestyles or competition in dressing. We were all expected to look equal and behave as equals in conforming to all the rules.

My head spins sometimes when I observe what happens these days in high schools among girls. Hairstyles, expensive designer clothing, matric dance requirements and expectations exert tremendous pressure on children who come from financially disadvantaged communities. Life with the nuns in the Catholic school accommodated everyone, rich or poor. We were only focused on discipline and education.

CHAPTER 8

Mixed Family Reactions to My Journey to Success

"Am I a white sheep or the black sheep of the family?" That question surfaced frequently during my journey, but fortunately it never derailed me from moving on. I faced the challenges head on.

Being the first female graduate in the family exposed me to a variety of reactions. Some positive reactions made me feel like a white sheep and the negative ones made me feel like the black sheep. I have, however, outgrown all of that and discovered that self-affirmation was the key. There is nobody who can affirm you better than yourself.

In my extended family circles, the reactions started as early as during my high school days. A close elderly relative later disclosed to me that I was not allowed by my parents to visit her house during school holidays because her children were not educated. She said my parents feared that her children would either pollute me or that her children were not a good match for me to interact with. The most painful part was that I could not share such utterances with my parents, as I would contribute towards further family conflicts.

Another problem was that in spite of the frequent bad experiences with family members, I could not cut cultural ties with them. They were and still are my family. We had been inducted into a system where children had no voice and were not allowed to gossip or to bad-mouth other adults, especially family members.

A senior member of my family, one of the traditional elders, once alleged that he saw me consume a bottle of whisky during my farewell party celebrating my departure for America on an exchange program. The funny thing was that at the time of the allegation, I was a teetotaler who only occasionally took some wine to socialize. This was obviously a smear campaign and there was much more such malicious hearsay.

The allegation was slightingly made to my father and he was devastated; I was his pride and joy. He knew only about my wine-drinking pattern but had now been told that I was a drunkard who would land nowhere in life. According to them, on the day of the party I had imbibed a full bottle of whiskey on my own. The irony was that on that particular day, I had yet to taste or sip a drop of wine.

These negative utterances devastated me, but I turned them into challenges on my road to success. I kept saying to myself, "If God is on my side, then a human being will not stop me." I have a goal in life and I will not stop until I reach that goal.

I am reminded of the following words sung by the American couple Bill and Renee Morris:

> "If God be for me, tell me,
>
> Who in the world can be against me?
>
> In the darkness of night,
>
> He is the light that shines within me.
>
> I will not fear. I'm not alone.
>
> He is my Father, and He calls me His own.
>
> If God be for me, tell me,
>
> Who in the world can be against me?"
>
> (The theme of this song is from the Bible, *Romans*, Chapter 8, Verse 31)

I believe strongly that God created me for a purpose. That belief propelled me on, even when I encountered difficulties or barriers.

It has taken almost my whole lifetime to work through some of my relationships, including those with several of my siblings. There were perceptions that I was unjustifiably over-recognized and acknowledged, that I needed to be reminded of my inferior position as a female.

On the other hand, it was not all dark and gloomy. There were positive experiences of support, respect and pride with other family members, including my siblings. And this group actually also propelled me on. Unfortunately, my parents died early while I was still climbing the ladder towards my success. Nevertheless, I know they died proud of my progress. My mother passed on after I had at least obtained my junior degree, and my father enjoyed watching me obtain the honors degree in social work. I took many other courses that were not social-work related, and as a result I coped with management duties, since I was multi-skilled.

I have retired from a routine job, but I am not throwing in the towel.

The support from my parents enabled me to go to the U.S.A. for five months on a professional exchange program, leaving my four-year-old son with them. Without their support and assistance, I would not have been exposed to such an enriching and meaningful experience, one that opened my eyes and brain to further development and greater aspirational heights. I kept reading and tackling higher positions at work.

I finally stopped on my own, having realized my dreams, and succumbed to the challenges posed by ill health. I decided to slow down and make my health a priority. I have retired from a routine job, but I am not throwing in the towel. I am now in the last phase of my productive life and exploring possibilities of working at my own pace, exerting less pressure on my health and within the comfort of my home.

Both the positive and negative family reactions contributed towards making me who I am. The external factors, positive and negative experiences, never swayed me from self-actualization.

I am registered to run my own private practice and hope that I shall apply the experiences accumulated throughout my life towards a fruitful and productive senior-citizenship contribution to the uplifting of communities. I am rendering counseling services to individuals and groups with psychosocial problems and also attending courses to update my counseling skills. A social worker never retires!

CHAPTER 9

In Conflict
with Religion

To anybody who is not Catholic, this may not make sense. It could be that only Catholics will identify with the challenges I have faced by being one.

Maybe I lived a life of sin, but the Day of Judgment will reveal my disposition. I was born and bred into a Catholic home. My mother converted to Catholicism because of marriage to my father—in line with the practice that you either get married to a fellow Catholic or the partner must be willing to cross over from his or her church to yours—and became a teacher at a Catholic school. My father had had to be Catholic in order to gain admission into a Catholic boarding school and his father had to be a Catholic parent for my father to be baptized and confirmed in the Church. My paternal grandmother remained in the Methodist Church.

As I grew up, I could not understand why the Catholic Church encouraged population explosion and increased poverty by disallowing its members from practicing family planning. I watched as most of the Catholic black families in the township kept on increasing the number of children up to eight, ten and even twelve, often without sufficient means to support them.

I grew up in a family where nine children were born, although two of them died when they were about two-years-old. It was a challenge for my parents to provide for all of us. The observations I made influenced me so much that I made resolutions around my own life to break this cycle of having so many children. It is interesting to observe that I have two children and both sisters have two each. I do not know why they made their decisions, but I know why I made mine. Catholocism clearly condemns family planning and divorce.

> *Despite my religion, I practiced family planning throughout my sexually active and married life.*

I attended Catholic schools from Sub A to matric under nuns, and this cemented the Catholic notion of right and wrong. Despite my religion, I practiced family planning throughout my sexually active and married life, and I controlled when to have children. I ended up with two: a boy and a girl, and stopped. I will never know if I was maybe meant to have more children.

The next conflict I had was that I divorced twice; and again, this was a deviation from what the Church preached and enforced. The dilemma I have is that I might feel guilty if I leave the Catholic Church now and join another faith with more liberal and accommodating conditions. For my own mental heath and spiritual peace of mind, I am still a Catholic. I have no experience with any other religion.

I basically glide along as a Catholic and regard myself as a staunch one, but deep inside, I know that I am not an "ideal" representative of my faith. I have deviated from the Catholic norms. I only survive because I tell myself that there is a bigger connection with a God who knows why we do things and is forever ready to forgive us.

As a result of all my "renegade" behavior, I find it difficult to go for confession. Occasionally, I do, but find it more comfortable to talk to God and ask directly for His forgiveness and deeper understanding.

CHAPTER 10

Gunfire and Smoke While Giving Birth

It was about 9:00 in the morning and I was screaming, "Nurse, nurse!" I was in labor and had been admitted to the labor ward of the Baragwanath hospital the night before.

This was on the 16th of June, 1976, when the first riots by the black youth of South Africa against the use of the Afrikaans language (the tongue of the ruling party during the apartheid government) had started.

I had gone into hospital the evening before the riots at about 7:00, and it was a nightlong period of labor pains. This was the first time I was to give birth and had not budgeted for such intense discomfort. I had listened to conversations about labor pains but did not expect them to be so severe.

In any case, no nurse stopped to check on me despite my screaming for attention. There was simply pandemonium as nurses ran back and forth past me. It was not until one of the doctors heard me screaming, checked in on my situation and shouted to nurses that I was in labor that I was attended to.

All the theory I had been taught about what to do when in labor was gone. I was just groaning with pain. I was not aware that history was unfolding, not only around the hospital but nationally and internationally as well.

I gave birth to my cute little boy between 9:00 and 9:30 a.m. that very day. I was a mother, very proudly so, and extremely excited. Only after giving birth did I hear that there was chaos outside. Buildings and cars were burning, and people, including schoolchildren, were injured and dying. It was then that I understood why there was so much commotion at the hospital. No prior announcements were made by the youth to the nation about what was planned for that day. Everyone was completely taken by surprise!

An announcement came from the hospital that whoever had already given birth must leave, because the staff could not cope with the burden of mothers coming in to give birth and adults and schoolchildren needing medical treatment for injuries due to the violence. I phoned my then-husband, who struggled but ultimately got to the hospital to collect us. We were both happy for the new arrival, but our concern was how we were going to get home, because there was fire everywhere as we left the hospital's gates. Emergency-service vehicles were also not allowed to transport patients in or out, as they were also being attacked with stones and homemade explosives called petrol bombs.

We changed routes several times because fire erupted constantly from out of nowhere as we progressed. I had to hold my baby high in one hand so as to show the youth that I was carrying a newborn, and raised my other hand to form a fist shouting, "Power!" My then-husband used one hand to drive and other to raise his hand in like sympathy. By the way, this was an instruction. Nonetheless, we reached my home and focused on celebrating my achievement: I had made my parents proud grandparents. After they had

His name is Tebogo, which means "a gift" and the other name is Stephen, after one of his paternal elders.

received *lobola* (bride price), the next best thing for them was to see me having a child. What a gift; having a boy was a bonus!

His name is Tebogo which means "a gift" and the other name is Stephen, after one of his paternal elders. He was the pride of both families and they all spoiled and loved him. A lot of people tried to coerce me into naming my son "Power," in commemoration of the slogan of that day of the strike on the 16th of June, 1976. Others said we should name him "Tsietsi," after the leader of the strike, but we had decided on the name Tebogo before his birth, so we stuck with it.

He now has a wife and a son. Both he and his wife are employed and live in their own house. Their son Lesego ("blessing" or "luck") is a cute little boy, too. As I write this book, he will be five years old and he calls me Gogo, the Zulu name for Granny.

The 16th of June is regarded as a major historical event and now a public holiday in South Africa. Known as Youth Day, it recognizes the young people of the country. There is no longer gunfire and bloodshed on this day. We mark it with music festivals, concerts, cultural events and other joyous expressions of our newfound freedoms. Of course, in the midst of all these activities, some will choose to consume alcohol, which occasionally leads to violence. But we thank God that it is now truly a day for youth.

CHAPTER 11

From Service Provider to Service Victim

After qualifying as a social worker, I was first employed by the State for five years as a probation officer. I worked with children under the terms of the Childcare Act. After five years, I moved to the Witwatersrand Mental Health Society where I worked for another five years with people who are intellectually challenged. I dealt with those suffering from mental illnesses like schizophrenia and depression, outpatients with social problems. I especially enjoyed working with people discharged from mental hospitals, assisting them in adjusting for return to their families and communities. This was described as the Reunification Project.

I performed a special study as part of my honors degree on the "attitudes of families towards their mentally ill family members, who were re-entering home after hospitalization in mental hospitals." I also worked with intellectually challenged children and noted the difficulties experienced by their families, especially mothers. Little did I know back then that one day I would have a personal first-hand experience.

I used to express unkind opinions about the parents of these challenged children for rejecting them. However, I soon realized that the problem was not with the parents. The problem was with the community's stigmatizing mental illness and ostracizing not only the children but also their families. In fact, the parents become the real victims because of these negative attitudes. People often behave as though it is the fault of parents that their children are intellectually challenged.

My daughter was born in the hospital after my visit to a general practitioner. Sensing that I had passed the date for my baby's delivery, I further explained to the doctor that I was getting concerned that I had already gone through two weeks of my allocated maternity leave. The doctor referred me to our local hospital.

I went home, packed my personal belongings and arranged to be dropped off at the hospital. Once there, I went through all the lengthy administrative admission procedures until I reached the doctor at the maternity ward. I was the only patient not yet in labor, much to the amusement of the nurses. I was a spectator as they ran up and down attending to yelling and screaming mothers in labor. I must confess that there was a lot more activity in this part of the hospital than I had ever given credit to the nurses for.

My turn for an interview with the doctor came and I was asked why I was there, since I was not experiencing labor pains. I explained the following:

> My baby was full-term according to my own records and clinic calculations

> If I did not deliver soon, my maternity leave would expire

> I was tired and beginning to stress over the delay

> I was requesting a caesarian birth, as I could not cope with the normal delivery process and pain

The doctor asked me why I thought I would have problems even though my first baby was delivered the normal way. I explained that I was young then (28 years old) and did not know what to expect now. The eight-year gap between the two pregnancies was long and I did not want to take risks. I was convinced that there would be difficulties and the doctor agreed. If I was willing to wait until after he assisted all mothers who were in labor and ready to deliver, I would have my operation.

I sat on a chair and listened to the nurses as they made silly remarks about my hospital mini-nightdress. Yes, I probably looked terrible; a big tummy under a mini, and tiny legs must have been an ugly sight. Just picture an open umbrella. I think that was how I looked from the front.

One of them said, "*Banyana ba itjha ka dimini*," as I was passing to the ladies' toilet. The translation is, "Girls are posing in minis in hospital." I just kept quiet, as I was on a mission and did not want to be derailed.

The clock ticked as I waited patiently, ignoring the nurses. For me at that time, the caesarian procedure was going to be less painful than the normal one, because everything is done while under anesthesia. My perception was that the pain after the operation was nothing compared with the pain of giving birth the normal way. Utterances such as, "There is no pain to beat the pain experienced during child birth," had increased my fear in taking that route, together with all the justifications I mentioned earlier.

As I was wheeled through all the procedures on a stretcher, I said to myself, "I am going into the operating theater and the next step will be walking out with my baby." My last memory of consciousness was on the operating table and being asked questions such as what my name is and why I was in the theater; I do not know what happened next, but awareness returned when I heard somebody calling me by my Christian name several times— "Letticia, Letticia!" I responded and apparently that meant I was back to life again. I felt the pain and it was awful! The nurse told me that I would be given medication in the ward to ease the pain.

The porter was called and I asked whether my baby was okay. I was told that the she was fine and I would see her in the ward. The porter came and pushed me on a stretcher to the ward. I was asked to roll over from the stretcher onto the bed in the ward; that felt like hell. I could not pick up my body and could tell that nobody was going to do it for me either; I was expected to roll over by myself. Nobody smiled, and the non-verbal communication spoke volumes. I grasped the frame and moved slowly onto my new bed.

I was shown my baby and told that she was all right; that was all I needed to hear. I had a baby girl and named her Kgomotso, which means "consolation" or "soothing," because she arrived after my mother had died. Her other name is Merica in honor of my mother. I was given medication and slept.

I had a baby girl and named her Kgomotso, which means "consolation" or "soothing," because she arrived after my mother had died.

Pain after the C-section interfered with my excitement and the opportunity for maximum bonding with my little one. With a normal delivery, where the major pain is associated with the delivery process, there is immense relief after the baby is born. This contrasts with the caesarian process, in which most of the discomfort emerges from the wound after delivery. Walking in an upright position is only possible after a few days; we called it the "dog-style walk."

I struggled quite a bit during the few days that I was in the hospital. Bathing and clothing a newborn were not such easy tasks. In addition, we were expected to be changing our babies' nappies. With my first child, the hospital discharged us on the same day, since that was a normal delivery. Besides, there had been violent national riots on that day and the hospital could not keep patients for long because of emergency admissions.

Tebogo and I had been discharged to the care of my mother and mother-in-law, who were both excited about being grandparents. My poor Kgomotso did not have such luck: she only had an inexperienced mom to take care of her. We were ultimately discharged from the hospital and told that everything was normal. When my daughter's development showed signs of later-than-normal milestones, it was my exposure to and experience in the mental-health field that caused me to suspect that there was a problem with her.

My concern and love for this precious gift made me overprotective according to my closest friends. My daughter's delayed development became a matter of interest and curiosity to some of my former colleagues and the nurses I worked with. When I left for maternity leave, I also left the organization where I was working with the mentally challenged. I went to work for another organization after having my baby. Employment in mental health abated due to funding problems.

For my baby's postnatal care, I was required to visit the clinics at my former organization. I noticed that my ex-colleagues and nurses were frequently in and out of my house while I was at work. Apparently, word had spread that I had a child with delayed milestones, and some of my colleagues wanted to confirm it by coming to my house to verify it for themselves.

On the one hand, I started wondering how mothers with children that were not only intellectually challenged but also had physical deformities such as microcephalus (small-headedness) or hydrocephalus (abnormal buildup of cerebrospinal fluid in the brain) felt when service providers themselves behaved in an unsympathetic and unbecoming manner towards them. On the other hand, I received a lot of support from my other colleagues and family. I vowed to give my daughter maximum care and attention. I exposed her to the best resources, which unfortunately were only in white suburbs; the black townships at that time did not have up-to-date stimulation centers or remedial schools.

Kgomotso is now 25 years old and attends a workshop for intellectually challenged adults. She has a good command of the English, Sotho and Zulu languages, interacts quite well with all cultural groups, and is very clean and friendly. Even with bipolar emotional tendencies, she is extremely caring and loves me to bits. I also love her so much because she is my special child, a gift from God. She is a beautiful young lady, and unless spoken to, her limitation is not so obvious. It has been 25 years full of challenges, but very rewarding when I look at her.

CHAPTER 12

The Ups and Downs of Being Single

I have spent more years alone with my children than I spent in my two marriages. I have been a single parent providing for herself and two children for about 32 years. I twice enjoyed the status of being a wife for a total of a dozen years.

Being on my own has had its challenges and opportunities, and those experiences promoted growth towards an enriched life, which nobody can steal from me. Among the positive aspects of being alone are that I have been able to independently manage my affairs; buy property and other assets; maintain them afterwards; and give attention to my children.

I think I am doing well, as I have never been thrown out of a house or had to face repossession of any assets or legal action because of debts. The things that I enjoyed most were:

Managing my salary and planning accordingly

Making decisions about what I deemed fit for my children

Maximizing interaction with my children

Developing outstanding multitasking skills that have enabled me to face all threatening situations, like the safeguarding of my property/assets and the protection of my children at all costs

Identifying, utilizing and maintaining safety and resource networks

Instilling moral values, law and order. My son has never been in trouble with the law and is now a 32 year old with a family of his own. (This I deem important, especially considering that he was born and bred in the volatile environment of Soweto Township)

Studying crucial self-development constantly (I acquired multiple skills, even outside social work: I did management, training, development and leadership courses)

The list is endless and my C.V. speaks for itself. I

even went on an International Exchange Program during my divorce after the first marriage.

What I find gratifying also is that I take responsibility not only for my achievements but also the failures. There is nobody to blame except myself for whatever happens. I had to deal with the following challenges:

> *I take responsibility not only for my achievements but also the failures.*

Occasional loneliness

Inadequate financial resources or provision

Lack of spousal support during difficulties

Disrespect from male-dominated systems

Bringing up a male child with cultural demands and expectations and the passing on of male values by a female parent

Dividing attention between children and other significant relationships

Professionally, being divorced also presents its challenges. I have refrained from seeking out marital-problem interventions. Being perceived as a failure in maintaining my own marriages would have been a negative factor in my efforts to gain the confidence of clients for relevant or successful interventions.

CHAPTER 13

Booed Down by Youth— Embarrassment and Culture Shock

We had a fundraising beauty contest for young people and the hall was packed to capacity. I was an enthusiastic social worker who had embarked on this event to raise funds in partnership with a group that specialized in organizing fundraising beauty contests. The group normally sought sponsorship from furniture shops, music bands and other big shops for prizes and stipends for judges.

As the host and project manager, I stood in front of the audience and asked whether we could start. I then requested that we open the occasion with a prayer and started the hymn "Re a ho boka More-na" ("We Thank You, Lord, Our King").

Some in the audience shouted, "*Haaaiii, fot-shek!*" ("F*** off!"). I stood there and froze. I did not know whether to sit down with the other VIPs at the table in front, join the audience in the front row or leave. I had been the organizer and accountable to Council for the facility and equipment and had to stay. I sat down with a forced smile on my face, but I was finished.

What embarrassed me most was that my brother and partner were also in attendance at my invitation. The contest continued and was otherwise a success. I was the only person with a black spot for the day. This was an encounter with the reality of the so-called Generation Gap.

I never thought that young people could be that ruthless, but I had learned my lesson.

All my events, prior to this one, had centered on adult women, who enjoyed starting the festivities with prayer, hymns or the singing of traditional songs. My judgment was faulty. I never thought that young people could be that ruthless, but I had learned my lesson. After that experience, I allowed the young to lead themselves, except for presentations that were of a professional nature.

I recovered with time. The miracle of healing must never be undermined. My emotional recovery was nothing short of a miracle. I now watch empathetically when older politicians address our youth on television and there is a conflict of interest. The attack statements and utterances remind me of that incident; my heart goes out to those adults.

What can we do? Times have changed and younger people have become more radical and increasingly vocal in what they do not want.

Anyway, my embarrassment was a learning experience that taught me to consult with young people instead of imposing ideas on them. I apply this with my kids and all other circles, and the approach has yielded positive results for me; it is, again, less stressful. Yes, I was embarrassed then, but this lengthens the list of experiences in the journey of my life.

CHAPTER 14

Robbed of My Parents Early, but Happy They Are Rested

My parents died very early, but I will qualify what I mean by the word. With the prevailing circumstances, however, I sometimes feel they are better off in their resting places than in this world of pain and suffering. My mother died on the 31st of January, 1984 at only 61 years old, nearly my present age. My father died on the 7th of October, 1987 and was 67.

I feel that my parents died too early, because I had not yet been afforded the opportunity to "spoil" them in appreciation for all their sacrifices, love and hard work in spite of the hardships of raising nine children with minimal resources.

Spoiling goes with having good financial means. Being a single parent myself and raising two children, I was only able to assist my parents in little ways where I could. I would have spoiled them to bits if they had lived a little longer. Each time I changed my circumstances for the better, like buying a new car, acquiring a higher position at work, buying a new house or advancing my career, I thought of them. I know how happy and proud they would have been to witness and be part of all the achievements and celebrations. Each time I see my age group and contemporaries looking after their parents, I envy them. I also deplore the fact that parents are often grossly neglected by their children.

However, I am sometimes of two minds in my thinking when I see old people suffer. I often say to myself, "Thank God that Mom and Dad are dead

> *I am sometimes of two minds in my thinking when I see old people suffer.*

and do not have to experience all the pain and suffering caused by the escalating crime, violence and gross insensitivity to the needs of older people, and even neglect and abuse from their own children and grandchildren." Also, when my youngest brother was hacked to death in January of 1990 in Soweto, I once more offered thanks to God that my parents were not alive to witness such a painful experience. May their souls rest in peace!

My mother was born to a family of 13 children—six boys and seven girls—of whom she was the eighth. We estimate that she was born in 1923 in

Vryheid, Natal. There were no proper official birth registrations kept those years. Although she was from a big family, too, my mother gave birth to nine children and I still feel that was self-battering. After we were all married, her greatest pleasure was in raising her grandchildren. She loved and spoiled them.

I feel that my mother only got to rest when the Almighty received her to a resting place in heaven. She contracted asthma near the end and an attack had killed her instantly. That happened at about 10:00 in the evening after being active and well the whole day. She had done her household chores, fed her grandchildren, sent them to bed and watched Dallas with my father. After the program she went to the outside toilet, had an attack, was rushed to hospital and certified dead on arrival.

My father never recovered from the shock. He was continually unhappy, suffering from heart trouble, mental problems and cancer. In 1987, he died while in the hospital after asking me whether it was okay that he ask God to take him, since he really needed to rest. I think he found it difficult to cope with life without my mother. In line with his wishes he died, but even as old as we are now, we still experience the emptiness of not having parents.

Nevertheless, we cherish the fond memories and the good times we shared with them. It was hopefully a warm reunion for them in heaven, and we do hope and believe that we shall also be reunited with them one day. I really wish they were alive.

There is a lot I would do for them to show them my appreciation for the life they gave me. May their souls rest in peace!

CHAPTER 15

Fractured Wrists

Another mishap! I fell from the stairs at work on the way to my car in the basement parking lot. Laying there helpless and afraid to look, I closed my eyes and prayed silently. Blood was oozing below my left knee and I couldn't move my hands. In those years there was a very strong need to stay away from blood for fear of contracting HIV/AIDS, so I thought that with so much visible blood, no one would risk touching and carrying me to the hospital in his or her vehicle.

A Good Samaritan finally arrived, a male colleague who offered to take me to the hospital. I had to be lifted by a few colleagues to the car and taken to a hospital in the township. Both of my wrists were fractured and had to be put in casts, my left foot stitched below the knee. It was nearly an amputation, but there was fortunately no fracture.

Life in that state was intensely miserable. I could not do anything for myself and depended on my ex-husband to help me with my intimate personal toiletries and bathing. This was an extremely difficult challenge, but I will forever be grateful to him for how he handled my situation. He made it comfortable for me to depend on him and I had a helper who assisted only when he went to work.

One of my female colleagues laughed when he saw me, joking that I looked like a teddy bear. I will admit that I was very offended at that jibe but I kept quiet. I saw her after I had recovered and told her that I thought she was very insensitive and cruel.

> *One of my female colleagues laughed when she saw me, joking that I looked like a teddy bear.*

After my injuries, my employer made sure that all the staircases in the building were fitted with rubber edges and support handrails installed. I fully recovered and continued with my life. Looking back now, I suspect that if that accident had occurred in the U.S., I would have received so much money from Workers Compensation Insurance that I would never have needed to work again in my life.

CHAPTER 16

Oops,
I Have Diabetes

I was driving to work when I had a blackout and drove into a stationary car at an intersection's red light. The driver of the car I had crashed into came out and exclaimed, "What a mess! What happened?" I had no answers. Fortunately for me, the driver of the car was a lady, because it was common for male drivers to get irritated and beat up female drivers for accidents caused by their victims.

When the police arrived, they understood my situation. If it had not been early in the morning, they might have concluded that I was driving under the influence of alcohol. They facilitated the exchange of driver information, insurance policies and other personal identification. Both cars were luckily only slightly damaged and no one was injured. I proceeded with my trip to work but was given time off to consult a medical doctor.

The doctor diagnosed Type II diabetes. My lifestyle had to change drastically, and to this day I am managing diabetes very well with the right diet, exercise, stress management and regular medical checkups. I have stopped stressing myself with questions concerning how, where and why I got this disease. Instead, I simply focus on managing it.

CHAPTER 17

Change in Societal Values

I grew up at a time when being above average weight was associated with good health, wealth and happiness. I was very skinny and will not even try to guess what my weight was during childhood. To me at that time it did not really matter.

I only became conscious of my weight at high school level while at boarding school. Each time there was a disagreement or conflict with fellow students, those my size, would be labeled as *meketa* (the plural of *moketa*). A lean dog is normally referred to as moketa. Believe me, that is not a very complimentary way of describing a girl. It really made me hate looking emaciated.

By the time I started working I was wearing either size 30 or maximum size 32. European size 32 is equivalent to American size 10. These days, with all the Western influence on African women, that would have been a good size for that age; but back then I was definitely not happy. I prayed hard for more weight and ate all the rich stuff. I poured mayonnaise on my food to make it richer and more fattening, but nothing helped.

When I was 27 years old, I was working for an organization that had a young, white staff and they truly envied me for being thin. They would ask me how I kept my weight down, and I had no answer because I was working hard to add—not reduce—weight.

At 27 *lobola* was paid for me and I knew that unless I gained weight, some of my in-laws in the extended family would not approve of paying the bride price for such a tiny daughter-in-law. While I was still staying at my home (after *lobola* had been paid), the uncle to my husband-to-be died, and according to tradition I had to go and assist with chores, such as making tea and food for people coming in and out to pay their last respects, and offer condolences to his family.

The moment I had dreaded most came one day when I came into the bedroom with tea for all the mourners. I greeted and gave them tea, and as I was leaving the bedroom I heard the late mother to my prospective mother-in-law asking whether there were no other women that my fiancé could choose to marry instead of going for such an emaciated *moketa*. The rest of them laughed and I was shattered. Going in and out of that bedroom was a nightmare, but I had no choice but to do it, and I could not share the experience with anybody. I resorted once more to prayer. Little did I know that my Maker would answer me only when my own outlook on life had changed.

The problem of being underweight went on until I became pregnant with my first child a year later. Even the doctors had expected me to have a caesarian birth because my pelvis might be too small for the baby's head to pass through. Miraculously, I gave birth normally and just had a small incision because of the size of the head.

I was looking forward to gaining weight after childbirth, but this was not the case with me. In 1984 I gave birth to my second child, my daughter. Still no weight gain! One lady said to me, "You look like *ntja ya moketa*," an emaciated dog. It was expected that women would gain weight after giving birth, especially when breastfeeding. So I did all the breastfeeding I could, but still no weight change.

Around age 53 I was diagnosed with diabetes and weight loss was recommended.

At about 50 years of age, things started changing. I began to gain weight and I did nothing to stop or control it. I was happy to identify with other women and engaged in conversations about weight issues, such as what to wear for different sizes and what to eat to lose weight. I was then a size 40 and felt good.

There was a price attached to gaining weight that had to be paid, because around age 52 I was diagnosed with diabetes and weight loss was recommended. What an irony! My dream of being heavier came true, but now I would have to deal with weight problems. I wonder why we humans are never satisfied with who we are. The skinny people want to become larger and the large ones want to be skinnier.

This was a wakeup call for me. I now started battling to loose weight. I went on different diets, bought belts to tighten the tummy, took tablets and went on "weigh less" programs. My weight fluctuated then, even as now, between sizes 42 and 44, and my waist moved up and down around 115 centimeters. I could not reverse my prayer, as I always remembered that I had prayed for weight and God had given it to me in abundance. What is ridiculous to note is that nowadays the skinnier you are (even at a younger age), the more attractive, healthy and proud you feel. Bone-skinny women even begin to get modeling opportunities. Today if you are skinny, your in-laws will see you as "celebrity" material rather than an object of shame. What a change! Rather, what a shame!

As I write this chapter of the book, I have a tight belt around my belly to make it a bit flatter. When I meet people who know me from my past, they cannot recognize the new me based on what they had seen of the old me. Even though my prayers have been answered, I try to discipline myself so that I do not grow bigger, beyond what I weigh now. My weight is not bad for a woman my age, especially because I do look after myself and say inwardly that I have grown more mature physically and mentally. All I have to do is to look after my health. Moving from size 30 to size 44 has been quite a move, but not bad considering that I am 61 years old this year.

I keep warning the skinny ones by saying, "I was also like you. Be careful not to gain too much weight because it is difficult to shed all the fat afterwards." They normally just laugh, thinking it is a big joke. They do not believe they will ever gain weight. I wish they knew me 30 to 40 years ago! My photos tell it all.

CHAPTER 18

Another Close Encounter with Death

I saw and felt death slowly approaching, and there was no running away. I could only pray and make hissing sounds. I have never made such sounds or felt my heart pounding like that before. One thing was definite: I was facing death.

I was part of a senior management team working for local government, and together with the regional director, we went on an annual breakaway to plan for the following year. The venue was the Pilanesberg Game Reserve in the Rustenburg area just bordering Sun City. The event was arranged and funded by the regional director for herself and the whole management team. We were involved in team-building and working sessions, but part of the program was to go on excursions.

On this particular afternoon, we were scheduled

to go on a tour to see wild animals, since we were in a game reserve. Three tourist vehicles, open at the top, were organized by the game reserve, so we divided ourselves into groups and got into the vehicles with a driver/tour guide in each.

Altogether there were seven in our vehicle. I noticed that the driver had a gun with him, indicating to me that it was a tour with possibilities of an attack. I did not share my concern with anyone but something inside me felt uneasy and made me think. Call it instinct.

As we got onto the main road to start the journey, we saw an elephant moving ahead of us and approached it from the back. The trunk and especially the head were waving back and forth and the elephant was issuing a white discharge from its backside as it moved. It ambled into the middle of the main road with no apparent intention of giving way to any passersby.

Our driver remarked that the elephant was in a bad mood and that it looked dangerous. The explanation was that it was spreading sperm and that it would do so for a distance of about 10 kilometers. Its behavior was attributed to the fact that it was sexually aroused and looking for a female. I was just about to ask the driver why he was following what he described as an agitated animal (because by nature, I stay away from anything looking dangerous), when the unexpected happened.

The elephant turned its head and saw us. Making a U-turn, it flapped its big ears and came running towards our vehicle. The driver never once touched the gun; I think he forgot that he even had one. He reversed the vehicle, as did all the others that were there. There was complete silence in the vehicle as everybody froze. The sound of accelerating vehicles as they all reversed was followed by my groaning and hissing sounds, as if I were in pain, but I never opened my mouth.

There was complete silence in the vehicle as everybody froze.

I thought of all my insurance policies and other valuable documents, wondering whether they were within easy reach. I tried burying my head under the seat in front of me, but there was no space, since everyone else had the same idea and seemed to want to die with their bums facing up. Maybe we just did not want to see the attack and were behaving like ostriches when they bury their heads in the sand in the face of danger. Just then there was a loud collision between our vehicle and another one as the two picked up speed in reverse.

After the collision, both vehicles stopped. Miraculously, the elephant turned and started moving in the opposite direction. What a relief! Maybe the loud banging noise of the collision startled the elephant, but it retraced its steps and continued to move in the same direction as before. Everybody took a deep breath.

I could not believe my eyes. By now we were

watching keenly, because the collision had made us change from burying our heads or closing our eyes. The collision was scary on its own and we all went to the bar after this experience. The first thing I did was to get to my room and tell my family on the phone that I nearly died. I vowed not to go on tour at any game reserve again.

With time I forgot and this experience became a joke. The following year, we went to the Nqonyama Game Reserve, again for a planning breakaway meeting as a management team. This time we passed by a pride of lions that then came near our vehicle. I froze as I looked into the fierce eyes of a lion and again prayed, saying, "God, if you give me one more chance, I will never try you again by coming near wild animals."

I vowed again that I would never take a tour to any game reserve. Many years later, I have yet to visit another one. I do, however, visit the venues, eat the delicious food and sit at the bar, but as far as the tour to see wild animals: sorry, not for me. Maybe I should also mention that after the elephant encounter, it was reported in the media that the Pilanesberg pachyderms were at the time the most dangerous bunch, and that a few attacks had been experienced. I do not know what the situation is now, but I am never going back there.

As I mentioned earlier, my journey through life is full of experiences, even close encounters with death, and this was one of them.

CHAPTER 19

Identity Crisis

Having to change from my maiden surname after marriage gave me a sense of fulfillment, accomplishment and pride. With a ring around my finger, a new surname and a man I was madly in love with, I thought the rest of my life would just fall into place. This used to be the dream of many young people: to finally get married, especially after completing school. Of course, things have changed now, for me and for most young women.

After a happy beginning, mother-in-law issues resulted in my first marriage lasting only five years. After the divorce I kept the surname for the next 15 years, the reason being that I had a son who was four years old when I divorced and whom I had to protect from undergoing an identity crisis. Tebogo and I were very close and we stayed together, bonding very strongly as a family of two.

My son knew and visited his father, who had already married another woman. Visitation arrangements for my son to see his father were very minimal, especially while going to school. They were most flexible during holidays.

During those 15 years of single parenting, using the ex-marital surname was not an issue, as my son used the same surname. My staying single all those years was because I had made a conscious decision not to subject my son at an early age to the pain of having to share me with a man other than his father. I had also observed in similar situations how possessive boys can be when it comes to their mothers, and how stepfathers end up competing with stepsons for the mother's attention and love. Some stepfathers even look for "spoiling" symptoms between mother and son, picking fights around these issues.

I managed this period of single parenting, during which I stayed and cared for my son, diligently. I basically kept one steady relationship and maybe two casual ones thereafter until I met a man who became my second husband in 1995. My son was now 19 years old and I told myself that he would now be able to handle any abuse, if any, from a stepfather, solving his own problems; he would defend himself and fight his own battles. My second marriage lasted for only 7 years and, of course, I was then using a third surname.

When I was with my second husband, people

would sometimes call him by my first marriage surname. Tebogo would also sometimes be labeled with my new surname, especially if the three of us moved together.

My son detested that. Remembering that boys are normally very sensitive about who they are, they will protect their identities at all costs. After the second divorce, the issue of that surname sometimes bothered me. I suppose it was because I did not have a child out of that union.

The worst thing I did was to wake up one day with an identity crisis. It was a feeling that left me thinking and caused me to go straight to the Department of Home Affairs to submit an application to revert my surname back to my maiden name. Perhaps I was full of anger and frustration, but I acted without thinking clearly. My decision was based on the affective rather than the cognitive senses. I continued using my second-marriage surname for many years until my new ID was issued.

The worst thing I did was to wake up one day with an identity crisis.

The strange thing was that the minute I checked my new identity document and saw my names and maiden surname, it just did not feel right. The following realizations suddenly came to me:

> There was no way I would be able to change all my documents back to the Mokgako maiden name; in fact, almost

all my certificates were acquired under both adopted marriage surnames

Insurance policies presented the worst challenge: they were all in the two marital surnames

Having to announce to everyone that I was no longer a Ledwaba (my second ex-husband's surname) but a Mokgako was now not achievable; it made me very uncomfortable.

I recognized that I had built up a reputation for myself up to that time. Changing my identity would cause me to lose my contacts and goodwill built over the years. It would also affect my valuable resources and connections for special favors.

I spent several days digesting this issue and the fact that my children would have problems convincing authorities after my death that the surnames belonged to me. The death certificate and identification document would complement each other, but the rest of the documents acquired throughout my lifespan would require verification procedures and processes.

I retraced my steps, went back to the Department of Home Affairs and reapplied back to my last marriage surname. I wrote a letter to explain why I applied for a change of surname. I now have my new identification document and am content.

Even after I returned to my maiden name in the identification document, nothing else changed anyway, as I continued to be addressed as Mrs. Ledwaba: only the ID had changed. I owe nobody an explanation. I am not a small girl anymore; at 60, I do not think I want to change surnames again. I have grown out of my identity-crisis situation and will remain with my last marriage surname. I do not think I'll entertain the thought of getting married again.

CHAPTER 20

Sonti, the Fortunate Kid

When I was growing up my parents were able to provide the bare necessities of food, shelter and clothing. However, we were still poor by every definition of the word. My parents could not afford to pay for the tertiary education of any of their nine children. Nevertheless, I was very fortunate indeed. I was able to go through primary, high school and university education with the assistance of external financial sources.

For primary education, my mother was a teacher in a Catholic school, and because the teachers were underpaid, the school subsidized children of the teaching faculty. This covered my education from Sub A to Standard 6 (Grade 1 to Grade 8). After passing Standard 6 I completed my junior certificate (now Grade 10) at a Catholic boarding school, and once again was fortunate enough to be subsidized. After passing the junior certificate, my education for matric (Grade 12) was also subsidized by the Catholic Church.

My university education was also funded, this time by the Catholic Bishop's Conference. Of course, my parents played a major role throughout. They helped to cover other costs such as transportation, clothing, toiletries and pocket money.

When I left university I had not completed my course in psychology. Therefore, I had to work and pay for distance-learning education to complete my junior degree. For my honors degree I worked and funded my distance-learning postgraduate studies. All subsequent studies were funded by my employer, as there was a subsidized-education scheme for local government employees.

Through my employer I did courses in management, training, development, executive leadership, HIV/AIDS and numerous other short empowerment courses.

I thank the Lord for having made the means available, given me the will and desire for self-development and taken advantage of available resources. I thank my parents for encouraging me to go on. I have in return served my communities diligently and unreservedly, because I believe that He gave me the means to go on. He had a purpose for me and that is to serve. The biggest fortune for me is having had a mother open doors for me.

CHAPTER 21

The African Ubuntu Lifestyle

ANguni word, *ubuntu*'s most important meaning is probably "human spirit." It describes an African philosophy of life and social conduct. Group solidarity takes preference over individualism.

I always wonder what happened to the *ubuntu* values into which we were socialized and acculturated from birth, of which some of us were beneficiaries. I am who I am today largely because of other people, family members, neighbors and friends to my parents.

When I was growing up, parents were not the only role players in the process of their children's socialization. I am sure you have heard the ancient African proverb which says, "It takes a village to raise a child." In my growing up years it was firmly believed that neither men nor families are islands; a child was a child to a community. Neighbors and relatives played a partnership role in raising the child. They were involved in any of the following ways:

Making a contribution, be it financial, material or in kind, whenever there was a need, e.g. during weddings, funerals etc.

When a baby was born neighbors would send soap for bathing and laundry, Vaseline, or any baby products to assist the family with the new arrival. I witnessed the contributions being made with the birth of my siblings, their christening events and during deaths in the family. I witnessed all these activities and have an even greater appreciation for them today, since I currently live in an affluent suburban neighborhood that was previously white-only. In my neighborhood most of us know very little about our next-door neighbors. God forbid, if I were to be ill for a long time and finally die, my neighbors would most likely only notice if there were many cars during my funeral. Some of them might even be irritated by the presence of "too many cars" and the flow of traffic.

I benefited mostly when I passed my Standard 6 (Grade 8) with a first-class pass. Friends, neighbors to my parents and relatives gave me pocket money, presents in the form of cosmetics, clothing, pens and other things. This I see as the perfect partnership, because my parents could concentrate on my major needs such as bedding, uniform shoes, night-

CHAPTER 22

The Most Enjoyable Phase of My Life

I just turned 60 years old and I am having the best time of my life. My purpose in life has changed and I now have some specific goals for self-fulfillment and gratification. Since leaving my job I have registered for private practice in social work and attended courses to upgrade my skills. I enjoy what I do, including volunteerism. I am also working in non-governmental organizations [NGOs] as a part-time social worker.

What is interesting is that I am doing things now out of desire and not because I feel a compulsion. All the hard work I have invested in this venture is very fulfilling, because I see the real me, the "hard worker and go-getter," and not the compliant drudge, merely acting on instructions. I do things when I feel like doing them. I schedule my days according to my needs and change my plans whenever it suits me. I wake up at a time convenient to me, watch my "morning-live" news in bed, have my four cups of warm water in bed, then a cup of tea. At my own pace I move to other activities, like gardening, visiting the library, reading, and very soon, seeing clients as per interviews scheduled.

If I do not want home-cooked food, I get into my car and go to a restaurant. I do not have to visit hair salons during their heavy weekend schedules. I visit during weekdays when they have less pressure and are available to give me all the attention.

> *I pray for an extension of my lifespan, God willing, but it is no longer a major worry.*

As mentioned above, I am also involved in professional work with NGOs on negotiated terms. I give myself space when I want and select which social group I want to be with and when. I actually do work on a part-time basis for two of these organizations and I derive much enjoyment from it.

The focus of my prayers has also changed. I pray for an extension of my lifespan, God willing, but it is no longer a major worry. I pray for a happy and easy death. I pray for my daughter's life should should she outlive me, and I pray for my son's marriage to be a happy one.

I thank God for the enriched life He gave me. It has been an adventurous one with good and bad experiences. People do not believe it today, but there were stages in my life when I would pray to survive until just the next payday. I was a single parent and had no other source of income. My monthly salary often ended long before the month ended.

What is interesting is that at this stage of my life, I now do things because I like them and feel good about them. For instance, I like looking good. I care for my hair and face and will spend lots of money to keep them in top condition. I do not do all that to please anybody or to be attractive to anyone. It boosts my ego to look at myself in the mirror with approval. I may not even be going out of the house for the day, but if makeup enhances my appearance, I shall continue to use it. I have heard criticism of older people for using makeup, but I say to myself that I will remain beautiful in my mature years.

If I feel good about myself, it even affects the way I walk and my carriage. Good self-esteem is key towards other people's reading self-confidence in you. You actually influence the type of response you elicit from people as you interact with different groups. This helped me immensely in my management role with subordinates when I was employed as a manager and in services to communities and organizations as well.

My social life has also changed a lot. I used to enjoy hosting get-togethers for fun or visiting enjoyable groups, especially with my contemporaries. I now enjoy a quieter life. I hate driving long distances or in heavy traffic. I tolerate social drinkers around me, but excessive alcohol consumption puts me off. I cherish having visitors time and again. I love eating out in restaurants, even alone, to observe and analyze human dynamics as people move back and forth; I always choose my tables strategically. I am at peace with myself and the world around me. I enjoy myself.

CHAPTER 23

I Am Still a "Black" African

There are certain cultural rituals that I practice, in spite of my religious and Western affiliations or criticisms from people who regard themselves as purely religious or purely Westernized.

I believe in God and His supreme power over everything and everyone, including the dead. I therefore believe that the deceased are in heaven, closer to our Maker, and that my ancestors intercede on my behalf when I talk to them. I hold that as people who brought me to this earth as a gift from God, they continue to love and protect me with the power that they ask of the Almighty.

I am a Catholic, and my religion fortunately recognizes and honors All Saints' Day and All Souls' Day. We make lists of our deceased loved ones and pray for them and ask the saints to pray for us. I practice all that, but in addition I periodically brew my African beer, *umqombothi*. After brewing the beer before I retire that night I burn *mpepho*, an herb that when burned to produce smoke and the desired aroma allegedly connects me with my an-cestors. I was taught to re-spect this process as sacred and refrain from reprimand-ing anybody or even getting angry. After burning the *mpepho* I ask or thank the ancestors or plead for mercy if there is a problem. During the night, the ancestors are believed to visit the house and quench their thirst with the beer, leaving bless-ings behind.

> *After burning the mpepho I ask or thank the ancestors or plead for mercy if there is a problem.*

My mother believed that if she had financial problems, the brewing of *umqombothi* and talking to ancestors could create a miracle that would somehow bring her money. So I was socialized into that way of thinking, and what I like is that it instills hope even under adverse circumstances.

Another common African cultural practice in which I participate is the slaughtering of animals, like goats. I have done this several times to celebrate my successes and achievements. I also performed this practice when my children turned 1 year old and 21 years old, and also during the acknowledg-ment of *lobola*. When my parents and siblings were buried, we also slaughtered animals for their funerals. I have felt comfortable about practicing this within my religion and I do not see myself changing after 60 years. I was brought up that way and feel that it helps me to cope with everyday challenges.

I respect the beliefs that other religions have and I do not criticize them. My belief is that we all experience life differently and design varying coping strategies without which life would be more difficult. I really do not care how my fellow Christians may describe me. I am a black African woman of Tswana and Zulu descent. I practice and combine both cultures and I am quite comfortable with that mixture.

When I miss my parents a lot, I visit their graves to pour my heart out or even cry when things are not going very well in my life. I feel that I can offload and leave the whole baggage at the graveyard. The next day, I face the world with a smile; life goes on.

There are other African cultural practices that I have chosen not to follow, but I have a mixture of Western and African cultural values that suit the way I live my life.

CHAPTER 24

My Unforgettable American Experience

I went to Denver, Colorado, in the USA, on an International Exchange Program in 1981. That was a very enriching period of my life and played a part in shaping who I am today, because it opened my eyes to look further than my nose for opportunities and potential.

The program was called CIP (the Council of International Programs) for Youth Leaders and Social Workers. It enabled professionals from different countries to travel to America, not only for a professional-exchange experience, but also a cultural-exchange opportunity.

We were placed with institutions and organizations relevant to our fields of interest so that we could interact and share different approaches with American colleagues while learning about interventions in similar work situations there.

Our education also involved interactions with fellow delegates from other countries. The selection of delegates for the program had occurred through applications and screening processes, followed by rigorous interviews.

Application forms for us in Johannesburg were obtained through the Black Social Workers' Association (SABSWA). I represented my country together with a male representative from Pietersburg. There was one representative each from the countries of Lesotho and Swaziland and representatives from other African states, Europe, different parts of America, Asia, and nearly the whole world as well.

The exchange of cultures occurred through our being hosted by American families. During my five-month visit, I stayed with three different families. The first family was a white single female; the second exposure was with a white couple and their children; and the third family was a childless black American couple. I do not have words adequate to describe the wealth of experience I gained during these short months. There was a crosspollination of knowledge and the dispelling of myths across cultures, politics and race.

I remember American children asking me whether Tarzan lived in Johannesburg as seen in movies, or lions moved around in the streets. I was surprised that even adults asked me whether I had bought special clothing to wear after arriving in America. According to them, on my continent we wore animal skins and walked around half-naked in the jungle, only covering private parts. I secretly wished they knew that Johannesburg was much more modern and bigger than Denver.

Life with host families was exciting; I was taken in as one of their own. They gave me shelter, food, protection, guidance and entertainment. I was part of their daily routine and participated in all activities. For transportation, I used buses to work and back. I was given all the guidance and directions by the families.

Prior to my going on this program I was working in the mental-health field, so I was placed at an organization suited to my training. I worked there for almost the entire time and successfully completed the assignment that I was given for that period.

What I discovered in America was that while I was content to be practicing professionally with my junior social-work degree in Africa, my American colleagues first went for their doctorates before practicing. I made up my mind to study further when I returned home.

> I made up my mind to study further when I returned home.

I completed my honors degree in social work after this exposure. After finishing, I continued to study, although I did not only concentrate only on social-work qualifications. The motivation for further studies was instilled in me by my exposure to the American Exchange Program, for which I am eternally thankful.

The experience with the host families was remarkable, because they were not being reimbursed by anybody for all the expenditures incurred while hosting. They did what they did for the love of it and to contribute to the success of the program. Time and again I drop a note and receive a note from my American families. I hope to go back and visit one day with my two children, next time at my own expense.

I intend to get involved in similar programs that need South African families to host foreigners. That would really gratify me, and I know that the benefits of that type of exposure cannot be quantified.

I recently saw an advertisement in the paper requesting volunteers to host students from overseas. I will definitely open my doors as soon as I get better organized. I know how enriching the experience is and it will be an opportunity to show appreciation for what I also received from my American hosts.

CHAPTER 25

Positive External Influence

My life has been a journey of good and bad experiences, but I am a person who enjoys introspection. I have used the bad experiences as a platform for better and greater heights. The good experiences became a source of and cause for celebration and inspiration to either maintain the status quo or improve on it. One thing I have always remembered is to not bite off more than I can chew. I always checked on my limitations and was careful to avoid having an inflated self-concept. For example, I know that I have limitations when it comes to technology and math, so I concentrate on where my strengths lie.

My career choice was influenced by my admiration for a social worker employed at the municipal offices where I grew up. Her personality, dress, job and general demeanor just told me that I wanted to be like her. Although social work at that time differed from the contemporary approach, the seed to help people was planted in me back then. Her office had supplies, like blankets and food parcels, that are not found in social-work offices today. I nurtured this dream until the choice of a career presented itself. I followed my heart and entered the field.

Although their decision was in good faith, my life's calling was nearly derailed by my parents after I passed my junior certificate.

The only profession followed by females in my family at that time was that of a schoolteacher.

The only profession followed by females in my family at that time was that of a schoolteacher. This was normally easily achieved through a two-year teachers' course after a junior certificate. There was also my parents' belief that a daughter had to choose a short-duration course so as to qualify for and be employed in a profession before pregnancy or marriage. To them it was important to quickly obtain a qualification, start making money, and perhaps improve later.

When I was in Standard 9 (Grade 11) two of my teachers approached me to ask what I intended doing when I passed. I told them that my dream was to become a social worker, but my parents wanted me to train and work as a schoolteacher. They did not approve of my parents' decision because I was doing very well in class and saw me with the right potential to complete my matric education and go further. The two ladies decided to talk to my parents, came to my home and convinced them to give me a chance. I am forever grateful to them for who I am today. I unfortunately lost contact with the teachers and have never been able to go back to share my success story with them.

The touchstone of my story is the ability of service providers to enrich other people's lives as happened to me. Those two teachers did more than teach in class: they made a difference in my life. My choice of a career was influenced by positive external influences, two good role models who supported me, and for whom I am grateful.

CHAPTER 26

Close Encounter with "The Big C"

The importance of support networks during times of distress cannot be overestimated. I have firsthand experience.

I have been very regular with my annual mammogram tests since age 45 and never missed going for the tests. However, I defaulted in the last year because of medical-aid financial complications. Three months ago, I went to do the test at Mulbarton Hospital, a private facility nearer to where I now reside. I had previously lived in an area called Glenanda in the southern suburbs of Johannesburg. In preparation for retirement, I sold my house there and bought another one in Mulbarton. This is also in the Southern suburbs, but much more tranquil. My new residence was the reason for changing the mammogram testing center.

After the mammogram test was done, I was told to wait for the doctor and knew that something was wrong. The doctor cautiously informed me that there was tissue around my breast, and when compared with mammograms of past years, the tissue appeared to be growing or enlarging. The doctor carefully explained that it did not mean that I had cancer but that they would refer me for a biopsy so that all doubts could be dispelled. He further explained that a biopsy meant that a small piece would be cut from the tissue and the laboratory would check to see whether it was benign or malignant, saying that they did not have the relevant equipment at the Mulbarton Hospital.

I understood what the doctor told me and was also very keen to have the investigation done. I took the referral letter from the doctor and thanked him. The referral was to another hospital, Union Hospital in Alberton. Alberton is a town southeast of Johannesburg with an inter-link to the city's Central Business District.

The Union Hospital told me that the cost would be two thousand rands. The next day, I phoned the medical-aid scheme, of which I was a member, to negotiate for financial aid and was told that they would not be able to cover the procedure. However, I made an appointment to go forward in a week's time with the biopsy at my own expense.

Meanwhile, I did a lot of constructive thinking and introspection, especially in relation to the financial implications. I made the decision to go to a government-funded provincial hospital. I asked myself, "If I have to spend so much money out of my own pocket at such an early stage, what will happen if the investigations are prolonged and have to be done repeatedly?" Since I had only recently retired and not yet had access to my pension funds, I had to be very cautious with my expenses.

I went to a local clinic and asked for a referral letter to Baragwanath Hospital, in the black township of Soweto. Baragwanath is a very large provincial hospital that was built to serve black people. My request was granted after I explained my need for the investigation and my medical-aid situation.

I knew that a visit to Baragwanath was going to be a day of challenges. There would be problems with parking the car, long queues and interminable waiting, but I was mentally determined to be as patient as I possibly could. A friend offered to accompany me for support and I really appreciated that, as I must confess that I was scared. I was wary of the process, afraid of the results and my possible negative reactions, and just scared for my future.

After driving around the hospital with my friend for a long time, we decided to park the car in the yard of one of the buildings and inquire as we walked. We were given wrong directions by some of the security guards. This is easily the largest hospital in the whole world.

We finally got to the relevant unit, but after standing in the long queues, when my turn for attention came, I was told that I needed to go to the mammogram X-ray department in another building. They explained that the X-ray department needed to do its own mammogram test and assessment. On arrival at the right place, I was told that the bookings were full and I could only be seen after three months' time. I allowed them to give me the booking, but I knew that I had to think of a Plan B fast. I was afraid that waiting for that long could kill me. The anxiety might trigger my diabetes and asthma condition and I could not allow that to happen.

When I got home, I spent several hours on the phone, calling around to seek advice from my friends. One of them was recently diagnosed with breast cancer and was handling the situation very well. I poured my heart out to her and said that the waiting would destroy me. The irony was that I was getting ready to provide counseling to troubled people in my newly established private social-work practice. How could I effectively do so if I had a pending unsettling issue myself? More important, I had diabetes and asthma, knowing that an unresolved issue could have adverse effects on my health.

Lillian Dube, a friend who was already diagnosed with breast cancer, listened to me attentively and I could feel the level of empathy with which she interacted with me. She encouraged me not to despair, because even if I were diagnosed with cancer, it would not be the end of the world. Lillian gave me the name and contact details of her physician, Dr.

Benn, who worked at the Helen Joseph Hospital. She works with patients who do not have medical aid. It felt like Lillian was my guardian angel who had spoken to me and given me the strength to go on. The next day I phoned the doctor's consulting room. I was told to go to Helen Joseph on any Thursday morning at 7:00 a.m. and would be attended to by Dr. Benn.

The next Thursday I was in hospital at about 6:30 a.m., ready to register, make my payment and relax. Even though there were several women, there was order and the service was excellent. The doctor arrived at about 9:00 and screened all of us. New patients were on one side and patients who came for mammogram or biopsy results were in a different queue. Other patients came for follow-up checkups. I have

I have never seen a doctor so caring, organized, energetic and so much in touch.

never seen a doctor so caring, organized, energetic and so much in touch. Before she sat down to consult, she mingled with her patients and checked all results and referrals. Her queues moved smoothly and speedily.

When my turn came and I entered, she read my referral letter and I told her that Lillian had referred me to her. She advised me to go to the mammogram X-ray unit so that they could do their own tests from the beginning. Dr. Benn had requested for an urgent investigation, but the bookings were full. The unit's attending physician, Dr. Rubin, explained that if I could wait until she finished with all the patients in the afternoon, she would assist, so I decided to wait.

At about 4:00 p.m., she called me in and did the mammogram and sonogram. She then called in Professor Joseph, who was passing by, for an opinion. Both doctors initially saw no need for a biopsy, as they indicated nothing worth worrying about. We discussed the situation and I pleaded for a biopsy so that I could dispel all possible fears. The two doctors consulted and gave me a day for the biopsy. The following week, I went back to get the procedure done, and in a few days time the results were out. There was no cancer and I was told to come back in six months for a checkup to see whether there had been further changes.

I went back home and lit a candle, knelt and thanked my God once more. I broke the good news to my friends, family and children. I will be forever grateful to Lillian for the support and her referral to the Helen Joseph staff for the good service, but to Professor Joseph, Dr. Rubin and Dr. Benn most of all.

To the women out there: please go and check your breasts through mammogram tests. Any early positive diagnosis can be managed and you will enjoy your life. Please do not allow health situations to stress and depress you. Go for help and surround yourself with people who will lift you up when you feel you are about to sink.

I am managing my other health conditions very well. I walk in the mornings, look after my diet and am busy rejuvenating while my contemporaries are busy aging. If I had been diagnosed with breast cancer, I do not think I would have collapsed. I had already prepared myself for the worst and was prepared to know the diagnosis so that I could start with all the relevant treatment procedures and coping strategies.

God has given me so many chances that it is no longer a second chance. I have had my share of opportunities and challenges from God, and I am grateful and thankful. In the past breast cancer was just a phenomenon in my mind, but The Big C almost became a reality.

Photo Journey

The following are a few selected photos that illustrate the story of Sonti's incredible journey:

*Sonti, matured woman,
matured figure*

First graduation at University of the North

At university

My late mom, Mamlini

My late dad, Josiah

Myself feeling good

My daughter, Kgomotso

Myself, Kgomotso and son, Te

Myself, Kgomotso and
Tebogo

Lesego and his dad,
Tebogo

My first grand-
child, Lesego.
What a pleasure!

Lesego is growing fast

Master Certificate
Training & Develop-
ment from the then
Rand Afrikaanse Uni-
versity

B.A. Social Work
(Honors) from
the then Univer-
sity of South
Africa)

My proud father at
my graduation from
the University of
South Africa

Traditional wedding
with attire from in-
laws as a sign of ac-
ceptance

Brother Eddie, myself and a friend

Brother Vincent, myself and sister Tshidi

Nice to celebrate my 50th birthday

Happy 60th birthday, Granny!

Sister Veronica on my right, mysef and paternal extended family

Reading of wreaths at my late mom's funeral

Friends Sitiso and Mumsy, and myself

Tebogo, myself and brother Eddie

Bongi, myself and Rene